THE NYACK LIBRARY

P9-ARF-447

THE NYACK LIBRARY

MODEL
BOATS AND SHIPS

D. J. HERDA

MODEL BOATS AND SHIPS

ILLUSTRATED BY
ANNE CANEVARI GREEN

A GROLIER COMPANY

Franklin Watts
New York | London | Toronto | Sydney | 1982
A First Book

THE NYACK LIBRARY
NYACK, N. Y. 10960

75557

Cover photograph: The
Charles W. Morgan by Revell

Photographs courtesy of:

Revell, Inc.: cover, pp. 7, 10 (top), 12;
Lindberg: pp. 8, 16, 17 (bottom), 22, 27, 30, 43, 46;
Entex Industries: pp. 10 (bottom), 21;
The Testor Corporation: p. 17 (top).
Photo on p. 35 by Ginger Giles.

Library of Congress Cataloging in Publication Data

Herda, D. J.
Model boats and ships.

(A First book)
Includes index.
Summary: Traces the development of boats and ships
and advises on building, painting, finishing,
and sailing plastic and wooden models.
1. Ship models—Juvenile literature.
(1. Ship models. 2. Models and modelmaking)
I. Green, Anne Canevari, ill. II. Title.
VM298.H47 1982   623.8′201   82-8394
ISBN 0-531-04463-7   AACR2

Text copyright © 1982 by D. J. Herda
Illustrations copyright © 1982 by Anne Canevari Green
All rights reserved
Printed in the United States of America
5 4 3 2 1

CONTENTS

Chapter 1
The Story of Boats and Ships 1

Chapter 2
Starting Out 14

Chapter 3
Building the Plastic Model 24

Chapter 4
Building the Wooden Model 33

Chapter 5
Painting and Finishing Your Models 38

Chapter 6
Radio Control: The Ultimate in Racing and Sailing 49

Appendix 55

Glossary 58

Index 61

MODEL
BOATS AND SHIPS

CHAPTER 1

THE STORY OF BOATS AND SHIPS

It could have happened on the Nile River in Egypt or on Southwest Asia's mighty Euphrates River. No one is quite sure where. But one thing is certain. It was one of the most important discoveries ever made.

Well before the year 6000 B.C. someone waded into the river to bathe or to cool off after a hot, dry day. Suddenly, a large log veered around a bend and headed downstream toward the person. As the log approached, the bather grabbed onto it, perhaps out of self-defense. As if by magic, it swept the bather off the sandy bottom of the river. With its passenger clinging to it, the log floated far downstream. And so the very first boat came into being.

Certainly that log was a far cry from the modern ships and boats that ply the lakes, rivers, and oceans of the world today. But it was no less important. In fact, it was probably the first time a human being had traveled anywhere by any means other than on foot!

Surely the discovery of the log boat was important, but it was probably not unique. Within a very short time, people around the world seemed to have made similar discoveries. By clutching a floating object, they could be transported from one spot to another. And they could do so without using much human energy.

Of course, river travel had its drawbacks. When these early water travelers arrived at their destinations downstream and tried to return home, they must have discovered very quickly that a river's currents flow in only one direction. Surely there were some sad faces and tired feet as the early sailing pioneers completed the long walk back to their homes!

A long time probably passed before the first attempts were made to build a better boat. The first boat to come along after the simple floating log was a dugout canoe. It was made by hollowing out the top of a single log. The traveler had a place to sit and a place to put his or her legs so that they wouldn't dangle down in the water.

Most likely, the earliest dugout canoes were made by setting fire to a log and then putting the fire out before it burned all the way through. Then, using a sharp stone as a tool, the charred wood was scraped away from the solid, unburned wood, leaving a heavy, bulky, but floatable canoe.

In other parts of the world, different craft evolved. One was the *coracle*, which consisted of animal skins stretched to cover a framework of wood or stiff reeds. Coracles were especially popular wherever there were no large trees from which to hollow a dugout canoe.

Another popular early boat was the Egyptian papyrus raft. It was built from bundles of papyrus reeds found growing near the Nile. The reeds were tied together to form a large mat. This mat floated when placed in the water. Large mats, or rafts, could support the weight of several people without sinking. Egyptian rafts were used for many years to move both people and goods down the rivers of Egypt and its neighboring countries.

Regardless of their shape and size, all early boats had one thing in common: they could only be used on water with a current, or continuous flow. If placed in a large pond or on a still lake, they could float, but they couldn't *go* any-where.

Eventually, someone had the idea to take a long pole aboard the boat or raft. The pole was used to push against the shoreline or the bottom of the lake. The craft could then be moved by pole power, regardless of the current.

Soon after that, the paddle was invented. It had a wide blade at one end and a narrower handle at the other end. With it, travelers could paddle their craft across the stillest of lakes—and even upstream *against* a slow current—in a very short time.

As people gained experience in piloting crude boats, small changes were made that increased their usefulness. Before too long, someone thought of stretching animal skins out on wooden strips fastened together. When this crude sail was lifted up to catch the wind, a boat could skitter across water faster than ever.

By 2700 B.C., the Egyptians were building boats from nar-row wooden planking, probably cut from acacia and syca-more trees, the only trees to grow along the Nile River. A wooden boat, though heavier than one made of reeds, was sturdier and could be built larger to accommodate more people and cargo.

It wasn't long after that that the Phoenicians, a tribe of people living near the eastern shore of the Mediterranean Sea, were building ships patterned after the wooden Egyp-tian models. The Phoenicians sailed their ships around the Mediterranean, powering their craft by both sail and oars. On board were goods and often soldiers, whose job it was to conquer foreign tribes. By 500 B.C. these first warships were feared, and copied, by people from many different cul-tures.

The first major expeditions by seafaring people came when Scandinavian ships crossed the English Channel to raid and plunder the British Isles. The ships were very long and narrow and could slide through even heavy seas with relative ease. As shipbuilding developed into a science, these Scandinavian ships grew larger and larger, and the first Viking warships were born.

The Viking ships were awesome. They were much more advanced in design than earlier boats and ships found throughout the world. When England's Alfred the Great saw them around A.D. 897, he decided to build several himself. And when the Vikings gathered a fleet of warriors and sailed against England, Alfred's own ships, called Dragon Ships, went out to meet them. The English ships had heavily armed sailors aboard, and the first great battle of the seas took place. England repelled the Scandinavian invaders. It was the beginning of modern naval combat.

Ships remained basically the same over the next several hundred years. By about A.D. 1200, however, English ships had developed into shorter, squatter cargo vessels. Their main function was to travel to foreign ports and pick up spices, textiles, and other goods to take home to England. They also carried English explorers to new and exciting lands, which England hoped to make part of its newly emerging empire.

Over the next several centuries, England, Spain, and Portugal continued developing fast, seaworthy ships to aid in the discovery and colonization of new lands. Often, in their efforts to claim lands for their own country, ships of one nation would clash with those of another. Soon, the English cargo ships were being built for speed, to outrun the Spanish and Portuguese vessels, and for war. The English no longer put a *forecastle* (fo'c'sle) on their ships because the high sides of the forecastle caught the wind and made maneuvering the ships at sea difficult.

On each side of the *quarterdeck* (the stern, or rear, of the upper deck), the English ships began carrying several light cannon, with more light guns on the main deck. These were used for firing stones or small shot at enemy ships and also to warn foreign vessels away from an area. The main weapons, though, were the heavy guns on both sides of the ship, just above the waterline. Many of these ships carried sixteen to thirty-two cannons, although in time it was not uncommon to find a ship with as many as sixty to two hundred guns aboard. These English ships were truly awesome.

With their superior design, speed, and firepower, it was only a matter of time until England overtook Spain and Portugal in their battle for sea supremacy. By the seventeenth century, the English navy was the finest and most envied in the world.

The eighteenth century saw very little peace in Europe. This was the time of the Napoleonic Wars (1793–1802 and 1803–1815) between England and France. The short periods of peace between battles merely provided both sides the opportunity to build more ships and weapons. The crucial fighting during the Napoleonic Wars took place at sea. And that was to England's advantage.

France's great leader, Napoleon, may well have conquered all of Europe were it not for the daring and skill of England's Admiral Horatio Nelson. Nelson began his career at sea at the age of twelve. By the time he was twenty years old and a lieutenant in the Royal Navy, he had gained command of his first ship. By the age of thirty-four he was captain of the *Agamemnon*, a sixty-four gun *ship-of-the-line*. In those days, a naval skirmish would consist of several advance ships (frigates) whose duty it was to locate the enemy ships, and a fleet of many larger, more heavily armed ships that would form a solid line to face the enemy. These larger warships were thus called ships-of-the-line.

Nelson and the English navy beat Napoleon at every turn, mostly because of the superiority of the English war vessels and their well-trained crews. In the battle of Trafalgar on October 21, 1805, Nelson battled with a combined French and Spanish fleet off Cape Trafalgar, south of Cadiz in southern Spain. He surprised the allied navy by abandoning the old ship-of-the-line tactic and sailing his vessels in two squadrons through the disorganized allied lines in two places in order to divide and conquer. It worked.

By the end of the day, Nelson's ships had sunk or captured twenty of the thirty-three ships present, thus ending France's attempts to dominate the seas once and for all. Nelson, though, was fatally wounded during the battle.

The 1800s ushered in a new era in sailing. It began in Scotland in 1802 with the *Charlotte Dundas*, the first steam-powered ship to run regular service anywhere in the world. At first, steam-driven ships were mostly curiosities. Their steam-driven paddle wheels were used to aid the ship in entering and leaving harbors, as well as in sailing during times of calm. For other times, though, these early steamships were also equipped with sails and riggings.

In 1807, American inventor Robert Fulton built a boat, commonly called *The Clermont*, America's first steam-powered paddle-wheeler. He sailed her along the Hudson River from New York to Albany and back, a distance of 240 miles (384 km), in the amazing time of sixty-two hours!

Though most early steamboats were fitted with sails and paddle wheels, around 1833 an Englishman built a small boat with a propeller. For years the question raged about which was more efficient—paddle wheel or propeller. Then, in 1845, two nearly identical British warships competed with each other. The propeller-driven sloop, *Rattler*, won every contest against the paddle-wheel-driven sloop, *Alecto*. The paddle-wheelers were destined to give way to the propeller-driven ships.

By the 1880s, steamships had established their domination over the seas—but by carrying cargo, not cannon. While

Revell's elegant *Cutty Sark* is 3 feet (.9 m)
long and has a mahogany base, brass-plated
pedestals, and cloth-like billowing sails.

Lindberg's *Robert E. Lee* is a classic paddle-wheeler,
which used to travel the great rivers of America.

some steamships, called *liners*, sailed on plotted sea lines or routes and on regular schedules, others would sail from port to port, finding their cargoes as they went, whenever they went. These vagabond ships were called *tramps*. Some tramp steamers like the *Iberia*, built in 1881, still carried sails and rigging, but it was used only in times of emergency. Improvements in the efficiency of the steam engine had made the use of steam much more powerful, economical, and reliable than it had been before.

By the early 1900s, the submarine was introduced and it soon became the dreaded scourge of the sea. The German U-boats (short for *Unterseebooten*, or undersea boats) proved very successful against the well-armed British warships during World War I (1914–1918). Though early experimental models of submarines had been launched, the German U-boats were the finest examples of underwater travel to date. Many were powered by inexpensive, efficient diesel engines. And their large supply of torpedoes proved deadly. In fact, it wasn't until depth charges (powerful explosive projectiles) were introduced in 1916 that England had any success at all in countering the dreaded U-boats.

After the war came of the great ocean-going liners. One exceptionally large ship, France's *Normandie* launched in 1932, used turbo-electric power to travel at the remarkable speed of 31.2 knots, despite her tonnage of 83,432. The *Normandie*'s engines cranked out 160,000 horsepower. Compare that to the average automobile engine, which develops around 100 horsepower.

It was all too short a period of peace in Europe before World War II broke out. The world's navies picked up about where World War I had left off, with the mighty German U-boats attacking and sinking British and Allied vessels by the hundreds. In fact, by 1942, German submarines were sinking about one hundred Allied ships a month. To turn the tide around and prevent what seemed a certain German victory

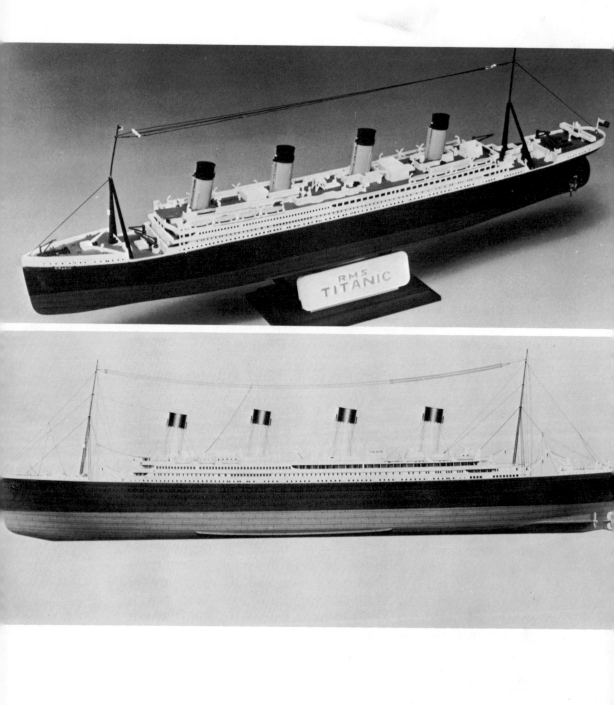

in the Atlantic, dramatic new weapons were developed. They were the escort carriers, small aircraft carriers used to escort convoys of ships through the Atlantic. Each carrier could launch and land up to fifteen airplanes, which were used to locate, and often destroy, prowling enemy submarines.

Meanwhile, in the Pacific, the Japanese attacked the American naval base at Pearl Harbor. Using 350 Japanese aircraft launched from 6 aircraft carriers stationed far off in the Pacific Ocean, they nearly wiped out the entire American fleet. The United States responded by building aircraft carriers of its own, newer and larger than those of the Japanese. And, below the ocean surface, U.S. submarines were sinking five Japanese ships for every new one built. Both above the sea and below it, U.S. and Allied naval superiority paid off in the Pacific.

Much of sailing history revolves around the movement of goods and products in cargo ships and the movement of troops and artillery in war vessels. But the last few decades have seen several new types of boats and ships develop— including power pleasure craft and racing boats. These are boats built for fun and for speed. Some are powered by high-performance engines; others, by a single sail. But all are part of the vast and complex world of boats and ships.

On April 15, 1912, the "unsinkable" *RMS Titanic* hit an iceberg, resulting in an unforgettable disaster. *Top*: Revell's 1:570 scale kit. *Bottom*: Entex' 1:350 scale kit.

Of course, many ships and boats—including some one-of-a-kind classics—are gone forever. You'd have to look long and hard before finding a real steam paddle-wheeler, the kind on the Mississippi Mark Twain used to write about. You'll probably never see a real dugout canoe outside of a natural history museum. And the great luxury liners of a few decades ago are all but memories today.

Yet these and other boats and ships from the past live on—in miniature scale-models built as a tribute to the history of our never-ending attempt to tame the sea.

Top: the *USS Forrestal* is one of the most famous aircraft carriers in history. This model by Revell has a highly detailed superstructure, radar antennas, cranes, and scale airplanes. *Middle:* Revell's *USS Hornet* carries tracker planes, tracer planes, helicopters, launch boats, and guns. *Bottom:* this 10-inch (25-cm) model of the *USS Arizona* by Revell is a memorial to the Americans lost at Pearl Harbor.

CHAPTER 2

STARTING OUT

People have been building model ships and boats for nearly as long as they've been traveling on water. At first, a sailor floating down the Nile River on a raft may have decided to make a model of the raft just for fun.

As boat and shipbuilding developed, however, model building took on a new, more important role. Often, by building and testing a new boat in smaller-scale model size, the engineer could tell if there were any faults in the boat's design. If so, they could be corrected before the more expensive, full-size version was built.

Even though model ship and boat building has been around for centuries, building a model ship or boat before the late 1930s was quite different from today. Back then, there were few model boat kits. If someone wanted a model of the *Mayflower* or the *S.S. Constitution,* it was usually built from scratch, using available raw materials, such as soft, easy-to-carve wood. Building a model was quite a time-consuming project in those days. Work on a single ship would often take a builder many months or even years!

In the mid-to-late 1930s, a few wooden model kits appeared on the market. At last a modeler could build a boat or ship with relative ease.

But there were still drawbacks. Model boat kits were limited to only a few models. If you wanted a kit, you had to settle on whatever was available. And chances were it wouldn't turn out to be a perfect replica of the ship it was supposed to look like.

Also, a wooden model kit usually contained nothing more than a block of wood, a set of sticks and, if you were lucky, a difficult-to-follow plan. All marking, cutting, and assembling was up to the modeler.

But wooden model kits were a step in the right direction. With skill, a boat modeler could build a model in anywhere from a couple of weeks to several months, depending upon the builder's experience and the complexity of the model.

It wasn't until the late 1940s that the first plastic ship and boat kits appeared around the country. Today, there are literally thousands of different types of kits available, along with more than an estimated one million ship and boat model builders in America, alone.

One of the nice things about working on a model from a kit is that you can follow the assembly instructions to the letter and be pretty sure of arriving at the exact model you want. In many scale model kits, the detail of the component parts is exact, down to the number of rivets in the ship's hull.

Of course, not all models come in kits, and not all are tabletop models. When people talk about model ships and boats, they may mean non-motorized tabletop models, called *static models,* or they may mean motorized models that move through the water on their own power. They may even mean ships with sails—motorless models, but models that nonetheless move through the water with a little help from the wind.

You can begin your own model collection of ships and boats with motorized or static models, tabletop collectibles that are pretty to look at, or floating replicas of still-function-

If you're into classic or period sailing ships, you might like (clockwise, from top left) Lindberg's *Santa Maria*, *HMS Victory*, *HMS Bounty* or *Flying Cloud Clipper*.

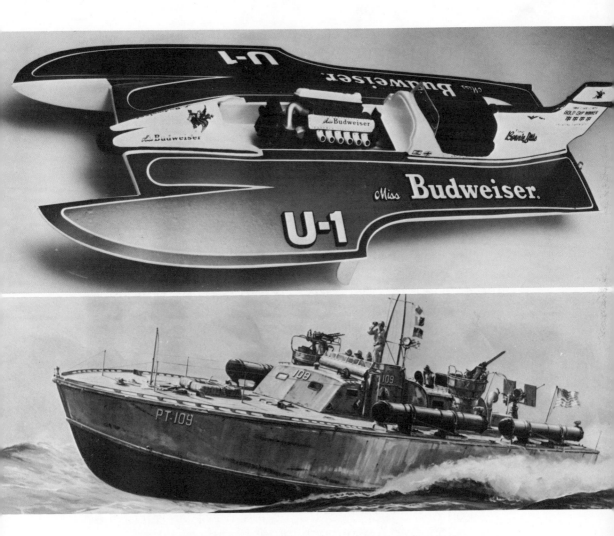

Top: for pure speed, nothing can beat Testors'
"Miss Budweiser" hydroplane. *Bottom:* one of Lindberg's
most popular motorized models is the *PT-109*.

ing ships and boats. It's up to you. You can get started building static models for as little as $3 (although some static models may cost as much as $350 or more).

As a rule, motorized models are more expensive than static collectibles, although not always. Some motorized models, those designed mainly to be played with than to be sailed or raced in competition, are often no more expensive than many static models.

Usually, the larger and more detailed the model, the higher the price. In motorized models, the more complicated the running gear—the internal works that run the model—the higher the price. Many of the highest priced models on the market are radio-controlled models, called RCs. RC model ships and boats are powered by battery-and-electric engine combinations or internal-combustion-type engines. The engine is usually hooked up to a gearbox, or transmission, from which is attached a shaft. The shaft extends through the ship's hull, and a propeller is attached to the end.

As the engine roars to life, the gears, shaft, and propeller all turn. This turning propeller causes the model to move forward through the water (or backward, if the direction of the propeller's rotation is reversed).

That's how an RC model moves. You might wonder how one controls the direction of a motorized boat once it's in the water. It wouldn't be much of a problem if the boat were in your bathtub or in a small outdoor wading pool where you could simply reach out and turn it or shut it off.

Part of the real joy of RC models, however, is that they are designed to run in much larger bodies of water—small ponds, lagoons, rivers, and even lakes. The models can actually change direction while on maneuvers by adjusting the *rudder,* which acts like the tail of a fish. Left rudder (when the rudder swings to *port,* or the left side of the boat as it faces forward) propels the boat to the left. Right rudder (when the rudder swings to *starboard,* or the right side of the boat) propels the boat to the right. And human hands never come near the boat.

How does this happen? Each RC model uses a radio transmitter, a small device that is held by the operator on shore. It transmits, or sends, various radio signals—invisible waves—which a receiver on board the model picks up. These signals trigger a mechanism that causes the model's rudder to move right or left and, on many RC models, enables the model to speed up, slow down, stop, and perform a number of other functions.

Depending upon the power of the radio transmitter, the operator may be 10, 20, 50 feet (3, 6, or 15 m) or more away from the RC-equipped model. Yet, he or she can control the model's movement by means of the radio transmitter.

Like static model ships and boats, RC models vary greatly in price. Simple models with very limited radio transmitters and receivers may cost anywhere from fifteen dollars to fifty dollars. Others, more sophisticated and with more powerful sending and receiving equipment, cost well over three hundred dollars and are manufactured for the most serious RC boating enthusiast. Some of these more costly models are entered in various races held around the country. Others are used simply for the pleasure they give their owners.

Not *all* model ships and boats that can be fitted with RC equipment and running gear are sold with them included. Often, models that can be made into motorized RC rigs are sold as floating static models. Then it's up to the builder to buy the RC system and running gear of his or her choice and to install it in the model. You can get just the model you want and equip it with the running gear you can afford. And you can switch running gear from one model to another. You may have six or seven RC-controlled ships, but you need only one transmitter, receiver, and set of running gear.

Something that *many* model ships and boats share is *scale.* That's a word used to describe the size of a model in relation to the real-life (or prototype) ship or boat it's built to resemble. Scale is expressed in ratios, such as 1:24, 1:25, or 1:12. Occasionally, you'll find a model scale expressed as a fraction, such as 1/24, 1/25, or 1/12.

No matter how the ratios are expressed, the figures refer to the size of the model in relation to the life-size ship or boat it is based on. A model in the ratio of 1:25, for example, would be one inch long for every 25 inches in the life-sized version. Thus, a model boat in the 1:25 scale that is 8 inches long would be modeled after a life-sized boat that is 200 inches long (8 x 25 = 200). Or, a life-sized boat that measures 175 inches in length would reduce in 1:25 scale to a model 7 inches long (175 ÷ 25 = 7).

Model ship scales vary quite a bit, usually depending upon the size of the full-sized version that the model is scaled after. For really large ships, such as battleships and ocean liners, common scales range from 1:144 to 1:1200. For every 1,200 inches of the full-sized ship, there is only 1 inch of the model.

Smaller ships and boats, such as tugboats and cabin cruisers, are often built in scales of 1:40 or 1:50. Very small boats, such as dinghys and sailboats, may reach scales of 1:12 to 1:24. Usually RC models are produced in the larger, more nearly life-size scales of 1:8, 1:10, or 1:12, although it depends, again, on the overall size of the real vessel. An RC aircraft carrier modeled after a ship some 1,000 feet in length and built to a scale of 1:10 would end up being 100 feet long! That's a little too large for most modelers to handle.

The scale of the model ships and boats you select to build for tabletop display or sailing doesn't matter very much unless you want all your models to be in the same scale. You

The sinking of the *Lusitania* by a German U-boat
helped lead to America's involvement in World War I.
Entex' model is in precise 1:350 scale.

THE NYACK LIBRARY
NYACK, N. Y. 10960

Lindberg's Snap Fit models include the German *Admiral Scheer*, the *HMS Duke of York*, the Japanese *Musashi*, and the *USS Pennsylvania*.

may want to have a shelf full of models ranging in scales from 1:10 all the way down to 1:400. After all, the fun in modeling is in building and collecting, not in having everything in the exact same scale.

There is a rather serious consideration in choosing one scale model over another, however. Usually, the larger scale models are easier to put together because their parts are larger and easier to handle. There are exceptions, though. Some large-scale model ship kits have many more parts, including more detailed parts, than some small-scale models. If you're a beginning model builder, don't overestimate your model-building abilities. Choose simple models at first. They'll provide all the fun and fewer of the frustrations that come with building complex models. If you're in doubt about the difficulty of a certain model you're interested in, ask the salesperson for advice.

Another thing to remember: while most non-motorized static models require the use of glue in order to complete assembly, a few manufacturers make snap-together, glueless plastic kits. If you're not yet ready to work with plastic model cement, or if you've found model cement messy and difficult to work with, consider a snap-together kit as a good alternative.

CHAPTER 3

BUILDING
THE PLASTIC MODEL

Most modelers agree that much of the fun of building model boats and ships from a kit begins long before actual construction. Narrowing down just the right model from the dozens or even hundreds available at a particular department, discount, or hobby store is exciting. Think about the type of model you want—a tiny dinghy, a New England fishing trawler, a powerful whaling ship from the nineteenth century, a little tug, or the sleek ocean liner those tugs are often assigned to escort in and out of harbors.

Or maybe you'll find a model of a pleasure boat your father or grandfather once owned, or a sailboat you spotted sitting in a harbor or skittering across a bay.

Perhaps you'll want a runabout, a cabin cruiser, or even a houseboat. Or you may be interested only in certain "period" ships—World War I naval vessels, for example, or a turn-of-the-century steel vessel used to haul cargo on long trips. Of course, you needn't specialize in any particular type or era of ship. You can select the model that appeals to you the most from the thousands on the market.

There are a few things you should do when you get home, before opening the package. Find a flat, clear area for construction. A table—perhaps a card table—is ideal, especially if you can place it away from the flow of people.

You'll want to work on the model uninterrupted by people passing by who may bump into the table and upset the parts. If there are younger children in the family, you'll need a location away from their curious eyes and hands.

Your room, the basement, or the attic may be a good place. Remember that you may have to leave your partially constructed model for hours, days, or even weeks at a time. You'll want to know that all the parts will be where you left them when you return to work and that nothing has been bumped, spilled, damaged, or lost.

Once you've located a suitable work area, cover the surface with an old tablecloth or newspapers to protect it from the glue and paint you'll be using. Also, be sure to keep all toxic substances and small parts well out of the reach of little children!

Next, assemble the tools of the trade. These are the things every good model builder uses to create a realistic-looking model. Some of these tools vary from one modeler to the next, but a good basic selection should include the following:

Emery board, file, and sandpaper. These items are useful at a number of stages of model building. Files and emery boards (the kinds used to smooth rough fingernails and toenails) are valuable in removing the rough "burrs" that are likely to be present on many plastic component parts. And fine sandpaper—such as 220 grit, 320, 400, and super-fine 600—can be used to smooth glued joints. A good brand is 3-M Wetordry.

Hobby knives. Razor knives can be dangerous when not handled properly, but when handled carefully, they can be valuable tools in building nearly any model. Knives made by such companies as X-Acto can be fitted with replacement blades in a wide range of shapes to fit nearly any cutting job. Use them to trim rough edges and to make custom parts for your models as needed.

Tweezers and needle-nosed pliers. Often, even the smallest fingers are simply too large to handle tiny parts. In those cases, you'll need these tools for gripping and holding small parts while assembling and painting.

Rubber bands and masking tape. Rubber bands are inexpensive and invaluable aids when it comes to holding two glued pieces together while they dry. And masking tape can be used for the same purpose, as well as for "masking" or covering up areas you don't wish painted. Masking tape is especially valuable when you're spray painting.

Toothpicks. These are useful in applying small amounts of glue to tiny pieces. Sometimes just a drop is all that's necessary, and a toothpick will help you apply glue to exactly the right spot without smearing adjacent areas.

Scissors. These are handy for cutting out decals. Don't use them for cutting plastic parts apart, however, because you may dull or ruin the scissors. Instead, use a hobby knife. As with any sharp instrument, be careful when working with scissors.

Modeling putty for plastic models. This is a handy substance often used by experienced modelers to fill unwanted gouges and holes in plastic, as well as to cover unwanted seams. After putty has been applied and allowed to dry thoroughly, it can be sanded down and then painted for a smooth-as-glass, professional-looking job. Never use acrylic putties on plastic, though.

Spackling compound for wood models. This is the best substance you can use on wooden models to fill in surface cracks before painting. Just mix it up according to the directions on the package and apply it in several thin layers, rather than one thick layer. Allow each layer to dry between coats. After the spackle has dried, it can be sanded thoroughly for a smooth, professional-looking job.

Paints and brushes. These are necessary for applying

One of the most beautiful of the early clipper ships is Lindberg's *Sea Witch*.

finishing touches to your models. They will be discussed in detail in Chapter Five.

Once you've assembled all the tools, you're almost ready to begin construction. Just remember that a good model—regardless of how easy it may be to build—takes time. Don't rush the project.

Begin by opening the box and examining all the pieces in the kit. Check the list of parts to make sure all the large parts, such as the hull and deck, are present. Then look over the smaller pieces. These will normally be attached to a plastic tree. Occasionally, a piece may become detached from the tree and will be lying in the bottom of the box, so don't throw away the box without carefully checking for loose parts. In fact, it's a good idea to keep the box until you're finished with construction. You can place the partially completed model inside for protection when you're not working on it. The cover of the box—with its full-color picture of the completed model—is a useful illustration of how the finished model should look, as well as how it should be painted.

As the smaller parts are called for in the instruction sheet, remove them from the tree by cutting them away with a hobby knife. Cut as closely to the part as possible without damaging the part. Be careful! Remember that the knife is sharp, so always cut *away* from your fingers and body. That way, if the knife slips, it won't gouge your skin.

Ask an older brother or sister, friend, or your parents to help you while you're getting used to working with a hobby knife. And make sure the knife is never left sitting around when it's not being used. It should be put away, well out of reach of young children.

After you've removed from the tree those pieces you need at the moment, smooth all the edges as you "dry fit," or fit without cement, one piece to another. Push the pegs only partway into the holes, or you'll risk breaking them off, which will lead to problems later.

Always follow the instructions step-by-step. Skipping around from one step to another or assembling a model without using the instructions is a surefire way to end up with a mess.

After you have achieved a good dry fit, the parts can be glued together. Remember when using model cement that you should use only the amount necessary for the job—not too much and not too little. A small drop for average-sized parts at contact points, and a thin bead along seams, is usually sufficient. A bit of experience in this area will help you judge the right amount.

Most model cements are plastic-dissolving acetone. As you apply the cement to the plastic, it actually dissolves some of the plastic of each part and then bonds the parts together as they dry. It's similar to welding metal, and it creates an exceptionally strong bond, stronger than many nondissolving glues or cements could achieve. It also has a tendency to mar or stain plastic surfaces, so be sure not to get any cement where it's not wanted.

In general, a smaller amount of cement will form a better, longer lasting bond than a larger amount. If two pieces must be held together for any length of time while drying, use a rubber band, masking tape, or a clamp. Wait from five to ten minutes for small parts, fifteen to twenty minutes for large parts, and up to half an hour for very large parts before assuming the pieces are well cemented.

While you're working, try not to spill cement on your work surface. If you do, and fail to clean it up or cover it with several sheets of newspaper, you're likely to forget it's there and end up with cement on your arms, hands, fingers, or—worse still—on the surface of the model.

One word of caution about working with models that

Four popular Lindberg line models are the *USS Missouri*,
the *USS Lexington*, the *Scharnhorst*, and the *HMS King George V*.

require the use of plastic model cement. The cement dries quickly on skin. It's not like super-glue, which can permanently bond two layers of skin together, causing serious damage and even pain. But model cement can be messy and difficult to remove, even if you have cement thinner or nail polish remover available.

When working with plastic model cement, be as neat as possible. And always work in an open, well-ventilated area. Keep the cement well away from your mouth and nose. Breathing in the fumes for even a short period of time could cause serious damage to your lungs and general health.

Continue working on your model until all the parts have been assembled according to the instructions. Sometimes, the instructions will advise you to put the model aside for twelve hours or more, and then continue. At other times, you'll have to use your judgment.

Once you've set your model aside overnight and gone back to it the following day, look over your work carefully, noting any rough spots, seams, and unwanted glue spots. Remove them with fine sandpaper (600 grit works well).

How quickly you assemble your model will depend on a number of factors—how much time you have to devote to the job in any one sitting, how complicated the model is to construct, how many parts the model kit includes, and how much model-building experience you've had. Remember: there are no rewards for finishing a model in record-breaking time. The only thing that counts is doing the best job of assembly you possibly can. That means taking your time and doing things correctly.

If you should happen to make a mistake—such as assembling two pieces that don't belong together or putting a piece in the wrong location—it will be easiest to disassemble them while the glue is still wet. Sometimes, though, you won't notice a mistake until the cement has dried. Then the only way the mistake can be corrected is by the careful removal of the parts with a hobby knife. Don't be too upset if your error results in some scratches, gouges, or even holes in the model's finish. These can be covered with putty prior to painting the model. But the easiest way to avoid such frustrations is to proceed with construction carefully and follow the instructions one step at a time.

CHAPTER 4

BUILDING
THE WOODEN MODEL

Building a scale model ship or boat from wood is similar to building one from plastic—in *some* ways. In other ways, it's worlds apart. When selecting a wooden model kit, you have the option of choosing a very basic model or a very difficult one. As in selecting a plastic model kit, you can purchase a wooden model kit with all the parts you'll need in order to create a finished scale model.

Most wooden model kits, however, provide only the rough-cut pieces for the major features of the model. This means you'll be required to do extensive cutting, shaping, finishing, and detailing of your wooden model ship or boat before it begins to look like the real thing. This requires some basic woodworking knowledge and skill. If you've never worked with wood before, you're probably going to run into some problems.

However, many modelers enjoy building their ships and boats of wood rather than plastic. One reason for this is that a wooden model allows the builder more flexibility in finishing than a plastic model does. Wooden model ships are easily modified or changed. A little cutting with a knife here, a little shaving there, and you can achieve just the desired look. That's much more difficult (though not at all impossible) to do with a plastic model.

Another feature wooden model builders like is that many of the smaller parts of a wooden model kit are usually of cast metal. The combination of wood and metal in a finished wooden model ship or boat makes for a very realistic looking model.

Unless the wooden model kit specifies otherwise, it will probably not include a motor. And it may not be able to be modified to accept a motor without a great deal of work. (Of course, many *plastic* models are static models, only, and won't even float.)

Many other wooden model ships sold as static models, though, may be modified to accept a motor or engine and running gear. They can be turned into fully operating scale model ships and boats—even RC models. That's especially true if they happen to be solid hulled, which many American-manufactured kits are. Other wooden models were designed to accept a particular motor and running gear, and the instructions will tell you exactly what is recommended.

Of course, the ultimate in model shipbuilding is building from scratch. No kits are involved. But you needn't go out and cut down a tree from which to carve all the component parts for your scratch model (although some experts do!).

There is a cross between building a wooden model from scratch and building from a kit. You can choose to build a prefab model. Technically, this is neither building from a kit or from scratch, but rather looking around for various component parts and putting them together in order to create a truly customized model.

Why not simply buy a kit in the first place and forget about building from scratch? Many hobbyists don't like kit models because they're someone else's creation. The kit may well be the result of the work of one designer or a group of designers sitting around a drafting table and trying to decide how the ship you buy in kit form should look when you're finished working on it.

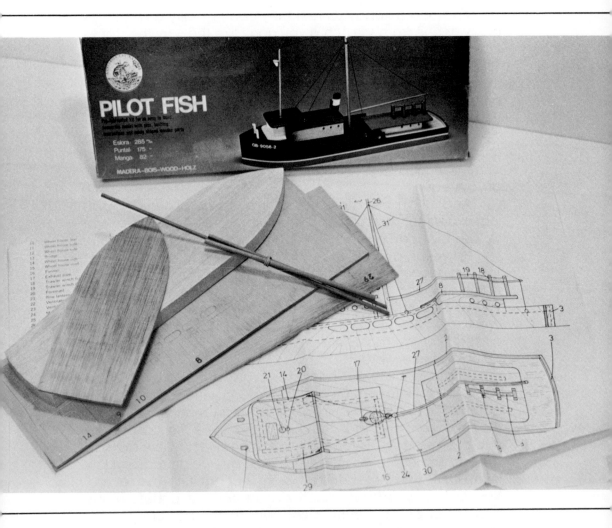

Prefab kits allow the builder to be more creative,
but require basic woodworking skills.

Also, some hobbyists feel they can't modify a kit ship as easily as one from scratch. If you don't like the way the stacks look on the *Queen Mary* model you build from a kit, what can you do about it? If you are building the liner from scratch, you can make the stacks you think look best. The ship might not be an authentic scale model, but at least it will be something you feel looks "right."

Other model builders enjoy the challenge of having to make or locate and assemble all the correct parts to produce a replica of a full-sized ship or boat, though that's not always easy.

And, of course, there are others who simply enjoy building experimental custom-designed models—one-of-a-kind vessels that can only be built prefab or from scratch.

However, a word of caution is in order. Unless you're not too fussy about how authentic your finished model should be, don't attempt to build a ship or boat from scratch until you've had plenty of experience building them from kits. Working with wooden ship kits is a good idea, as it gives you a "feel" for the material.

One more word of caution. If you can't wait to try your model ship or boat out on water, work from plans. (See the Appendix for information about where to write to for ship and boat plans.) Little is more frustrating than finishing a scratch model only to find that the *superstructure*—the part of the ship above deck—is too high or too heavy to allow the ship to float. Sometimes, a little extra *ballast*—weight carried low in the hull—will correct the problem, but not if it's too severe. You can only add so much ballast to a ship before she swamps or possibly even dives right to the bottom. There's little you can do short of tearing down and replacing parts with lighter parts if the superstructure is too heavy to allow the ship to float. Top-notch, experienced builders often use formulas devised by naval architects to find the proper weights and dimensions of ships or boats designed to float.

Of course, you needn't make the jump from kit builder to scratch builder overnight. As you gain experience in building wooden ships from kits, you may feel the urge to begin customizing some of your models—replacing a stack here, changing the superstructure there. This is an excellent way to get into scratch building—just a little at a time. Through customizing, you'll begin to get a feel for scratch building.

How do you assemble a wooden ship, either from a kit or from scratch? The building plans will most likely specify the best way. The instructions may call for some gluing, some nailing, and some screwing. That means you'll need a few extra tools that plastic model builders don't normally require—things like a small hammer, a screwdriver or two (in different sizes), pliers, chisels, files, and a razor saw. Sometimes a coping saw comes in handy for trimming large pieces of wood.

One word about glue: don't plan on using the same cement you'd use on a plastic model on your wooden model. Remember, plastic model cement works by dissolving a thin layer of plastic and "melting" the joined pieces together. For joining two pieces of wood, you'll need a good quality wood glue, which works by seeping into the pores of each of the pieces to be joined. White glues such as Titebond®, Sobo®, and Elmer's® work best. When the pieces are pressed and held together, a tight bond results.

Plan ahead to avoid disappointment when building a wooden model ship or boat—whether from kit, from scratch, or prefab. If possible, talk to someone who has had some experience in building the kit or scratch model you wish to build, or one like it. And remember: follow the plans.

CHAPTER 5

PAINTING AND FINISHING YOUR MODELS

Both plastic and wooden model ships must be painted after they are assembled. And, of course, if you've built a wooden boat you plan to sail, you'll need to protect the wood with paint, wax, or marine varnish to keep the wood from absorbing water, becoming waterlogged, or discoloring.

Also, depending upon the model you're building, you may want to add pinstriping, letters, numerals, or various logos in order to make the ship or boat look more realistic.

While some model builders like to wait until their models are completely assembled before painting, most prefer to do the painting before the pieces are put together. Usually, prepainting the pieces before assembling them results in a neater, more realistic-looking job. If you miss some areas or happen to scratch some paint off while assembling the model, you can always go back later and touch up those spots.

Before painting a plastic model, it's a good idea to wash the parts gently in a mild soap solution. Then rinse them thoroughly under running water or (for small parts) in a pan of clear water, and allow the parts to dry fully. It's not necessary to wash wooden model parts before assembly.

Once the plastic parts have been washed, try not to handle them with your fingers, since any oil or dirt on your hands will cling to the parts, preventing the paint from sticking properly. Use a clean pair of lightweight cotton or plastic gloves to handle the parts, or handle them with tweezers. Throwaway plastic gloves, available at many hobby and photo stores, are excellent, very flexible, and inexpensive.

Plan on painting the parts as soon as possible after they are dry. Don't leave them sitting around for days or they'll collect dust, which will then have to be washed off again before painting.

Spray painting is the most effective and quickest way of applying a thin, even coat of paint to your model. Unfortunately, spray painting can also be the messiest—*if* you fail to take certain precautions before beginning.

First, to prevent overspray—the fine mist that winds up floating off into the air—from scattering around the room, you should lay down at least a 6-foot (1.8-m) square or larger tarp, plastic sheet, or section of newspapers. Then, if possible, get a large box from which the top has been removed. You can use it as a spray box.

Position the box so that the open end faces you. Place the parts to be sprayed (all those to be painted the same color) inside the box. As you begin to spray, the overspray will wash up against the sides of the box, keeping the airborne mist to a minimum. To be on the safe side, do all your spraying in the basement, attic, garage, or even outside, if the temperature is between 70° to 95° F (21° to 35°C) and there is not much wind. The idea is to spray paint somewhere where a little overspray won't do any damage to the surroundings.

To prevent freshly sprayed parts from sticking to the bottom of the spray box as the paint dries and to make it easier to cover all sides of the parts, make a hook from a thin wire hanger and suspend it from the top of the box. To fasten the hook to the box, poke it through the cardboard, and bend the wire to make it secure. You can hang the parts to be

THE NYACK LIBRARY
NYACK, N. Y. 10960

Spray box

sprayed from the hook. Use several hooks if you're doing several pieces at one time.

As you begin spray painting, hold the sprayer from 8 to 12 inches (20 to 30 cm) from the surface of the model. If you're using a spray can, try to keep the can upright to prevent spattering and possible clogging of the nozzle. Most spray cans won't spray properly if turned on their side or upside down.

Spray in a back-and-forth motion until the entire surface of the part you're spraying has been covered lightly and evenly. Don't apply too much spray with one coat, or the paint will run, leaving hard-to-remove drip marks on the finished model.

Generally, you'll find that from three to five light coats of spray paint are necessary for a good job. Allow plenty of drying time between coats (check the spray can for suggestions), and only handle the parts—again, with clean gloves—after the paint has dried fully, usually one to three days if a hobby enamel paint has been used.

If you find working with a spray can to be awkward or inefficient, you might consider investing in a spray gun. However, spray guns are *very* expensive (in the $40 and up price range) and rather difficult to learn to use properly. Anyone can shoot paint from a gun, but doing it correctly, so as to end up with a first-class paint job, takes practice. It's definitely something you can keep in mind and look forward to using someday—once you've saved up enough money and gotten some experience in spray painting with cans.

In general, two types of spray gun units are available for a modeler's use. Both consist of a small gun with an adjustable nozzle to alter the flow rate and pattern of spray from pinpoint to wide mist. The gun is connected by a hose to a source of pressurized air. A small jar attached to the gun can be filled with paint and may be refilled.

One type of spray unit is powered by a can of pressurized air. Each can delivers from one to three hours of spraying time before it must be discarded and replaced with another can. This type of spray unit costs from forty dollars up. A second type of spray unit is powered by an electrically operated air compressor. This type of spray system is the more professional—and the more expensive—of the two, with some units costing several hundred dollars. It's actually a miniature spray version of the systems used to paint full-sized ships and boats. If you plan on doing a lot of spraying, it would be a wise investment. If, on the other hand, your spray jobs will be limited to just a few a year, you'll probably be better off with a pressurized can spray system.

Whichever system you choose, you'll find that the portable gun-and-hose allows you greater flexibility than ordinary spray cans of paint do in reaching hard-to-spray areas. However, you can get an excellent spray job from canned spray—if you take the time to do the job right.

Once you begin spraying, you can expect everything on the model to receive a coat of paint, unless you take precautions. To prevent certain parts from being painted, remove them from their tree or cover them with a piece of masking tape. That way, the parts you don't want painted will be protected from paint by the tape. And it's a good idea to mask off those areas that will receive cement, since model cement doesn't stick very well to paint.

Do not add chromed parts to your model until *after* you

From its foreign battleship line, Lindberg offers the German *Bismarck*, the German *Tirpitz*, and the British *Hood*.

GERMAN BATTLESHIP

LINDBE

have painted it. If paint gets on a chromed part, the chrome finish will be ruined.

There are several techniques experienced modelers use to mask areas to prevent them from being sprayed. You can cover up large areas such as a hull, deck, or stacks, with masking tape. Smaller decorative pieces should be left off the model until the painting has been completed. Then you can go back and paint these small parts with a fine brush.

Another method of masking large areas you wish to leave unpainted is to use a brush-on liquid masker, such as Magic Masker or Metalflake's® Spray Mask, available at automotive paint stores. It's a liquid you brush onto areas that are to be left unpainted. Allow the liquid to dry and then spray the model. After the spray paint has dried, simply peel off the liquid masker for a perfect job of color separation. Just be sure not to get the liquid masker on areas you *do* want painted, or you'll miss some spots which you'll have to touch up later.

You can't use just any paint to cover your model. Some paints won't stick to plastic. The most frequently used is enamel, which comes in spray cans and in liquid form for brushing on. Several companies manufacture enamel expressly for models. If you check at your nearby hobby store, you'll find a wide variety of colors to choose from.

Another paint sometimes used for plastic models is lacquer. Floquil makes a good lacquer in a wide range of colors. For wooden models, you can use either enamel or lacquer.

While you're buying paint, be sure to buy some paint thinner for cleaning brushes—for you'll need brushes, even if you plan on spray painting your model. Buy a good grade of thinner, or buy enamel reducer when working with enamel paints. Always clean up your painting mess as soon as possible. If paintbrushes and other tools are allowed to dry before cleaning, cleanup will be more difficult, if not impossible.

If the thought of working with thinners and messy, hard-to-clean-up paint doesn't appeal to you, don't despair. There are other types of paint on the market—paint which is much easier to work with and which produces good results when applied properly. One such paint is Polly-S, a water-based enamel which can be used to paint both wood and plastic models. Because of its water base, Polly-S can be cleaned up with soap and water. Hands, tools, and tabletops all clean up quickly and easily—*if* you don't wait until the paint has had time to dry for several days.

To clean brushes that have been used to apply water-based paint, run the bristles under lukewarm water for several seconds, and then apply a mild liquid detergent, such as dishwashing liquid. Rub the detergent into the bristles and then rinse thoroughly in running water. When there is no sign of color in the brush or the basin, the brush is clean. Use your fingers to gently "shape" the bristles, pulling them to a point, and allow the bristles to dry. Make sure you shape the bristles while still wet, and don't allow them to come in contact with any other brushes or containers, or the bristles may become frizzy or dry into a curved shape. The brush will be useless the next time you go to paint small sections of a model.

When buying brushes, buy only the finest model and quality paintbrushes. Choose good camel-hair brushes for painting large areas and pointed red-sable brushes for finely detailed work. Cheap brushes—such as those most often available at discount, dime, and hardware stores—will shed their bristles, leaving hairs on your finished work. Expect to pay a little more for quality camel-hair and red-sable paintbrushes.

When painting with a brush, try to apply the paint evenly. If the paint goes on too thickly, you'll end up with high spots, runs, and sags that will spoil the look of your finished model. If the paint goes on too thinly, you'll have bare spots and streaks in the job.

Plan on applying at least two coats of paint when using

U.S.S. YORKTOWN
U.S. NAVY AIRCRAFT CARRIER

WORLD WAR TWO
BATTLE OF MIDWAY

MOTORIZED
authentic scale model
plastic construction kit

LINDBERG

U.S. NAVY
MINESWEEPER

MOTORIZED
AUTHENTIC SCALE PLASTIC MODEL CONSTRUCTION KIT

LINDBERG

299

LSD **U.S. NAVY LANDING SHIP DOCK**
MOTORIZED AUTHENTIC SCALE PLASTIC MODEL CONSTRUCTION KIT

LINDBERG

26

a brush. The first coat can go on just as it comes from the bottle. For a smoother final coat, cut the paint. Mix three-quarters paint with one-quarter paint thinner or enamel reducer (if the paint you're using is enamel).

Pinstriping is very popular with many model builders. Many types of ships and boats, from decorative Spanish galleons to modern runabouts, are decorated with narrow stripes in black or other colors. While pinstripes can be painted on a model freehand, getting those thin lines on straight is very tedious work. It's much easier and more effective to use a product like Tapestripe®. It comes in a roll 75 inches (190 cm) long and has a self-sticking adhesive backing, like tape. Simply unroll as much of the stripe as you wish, apply it to your model, trim off the ends with a hobby knife, reposition the tape if necessary, and then burnish or press firmly when you're ready to make the stripe permanent.

You'll find several brands of pinstripe tape available at hobby, paint, and art supply stores, as well as automotive paint shops. They come in all colors from basic black to fluorescent and metallic.

Lettering is also an important part of finishing many model boats and ships, especially for military and racing models. You can buy decals to soak in water and then apply to your model. In fact, decals are included with many model kits. But

Three of Lindberg's popular naval vessels include the *USS Yorktown*, a U.S. Navy minesweeper, and a Navy LSD landing ship dock—all motorized.

decals leave a "haze" that looks very artificial. As time passes, they also tend to yellow.

Instead of decals, try using dry lettering. Dry letters come on an acetate, or plastic, sheet. To apply them to your model, simply position them where you want them, then burnish them off their plastic sheet and onto the model. Presto! You'll have a realistic-looking lettering job with no telltale haze. And dry lettering is easier to work with than decals are, too. Just be sure all your painting is done before you start thinking about lettering, decals, and other decorations.

Other stick-ons available at many hobby shops include a wide range of company logos, designed to indicate sponsors for racing boats (such as the famous "Miss Budweiser") and owners/operators of cargo ships and tankers (such as "Gulf," "Shell," and "Phillips 66"). Ask to see your hobby shop dealer's collection. And, while you're at it, check out the selection of brass fittings, military insignias, and scale-model boat figures. Used wisely, all can help your newly built model look even more authentic.

Finally, to prevent the letters, pinstripes, and stick-ons from wearing off or getting chipped in handling or racing, select a clear spray to cover and protect your model. The sprays available come in either high gloss or flat, so you can take your pick.

CHAPTER 6

RADIO CONTROL: THE ULTIMATE IN RACING AND SAILING

The wind comes up suddenly, whipping the water into angry, whitecapped waves. Just as suddenly, rain comes down in thick, menacing sheets. Out on the water, so far out it's barely visible, a two-masted schooner swings its sails around. The captain makes the decision to head to port, and the auxiliary engine pops and gurgles, then chugs to life.

The tiny schooner tosses and bobs on the waves, bravely struggling toward port and safety. Once there, the ship can ride out the storm in the shelter of shallow waters and calmer winds. But safety is still a long way off.

Suddenly, a strong gale catches the sail and the ship nearly capsizes! The captain gives the order to furl the sails, and down they come. Only the tiny two-cylinder backup engine keeps the schooner chugging slowly toward shore.

Is this a life-and-death scenario played out on the Atlantic Coast? It could be, but it's not. Actually, the ship is a 26-inch (66-cm) model, wet and battered but safe. The captain is an RC modeler, standing safely on shore.

RC (which stands for radio control) modeling is the ultimate goal of many model ship and boat hobbyists. Whether pleasure sailing—like the hobbyist taking the schooner for a spin around the park lagoon—or flat-out racing against an armada of competitors all built for speed, it's as close to real boating as a person can come without going out on the water.

Before you get too enthused about RC model ships and boats, remember that these are not toys. They are highly sophisticated electronically operated scale models, many of which are expensive—one hundred dollars and up. That means you're going to have to save a lot of allowances before you're likely to have enough money to buy an RC model. And you're going to have to invest a lot of time in learning the basics of operating a radio-control system before ever setting your model in the water. In other words, it's something you can work up to. But it's definitely worth the time, energy, and money if RC modeling appeals to you.

RC ships and boats need no wires, lines, or preset rudders. Unlike some motorized toy boats and models that feature a turning screw and a rudder you must set by hand, the RC model is a vessel with a motor and a "mind" of its own.

Each RC model is powered either electrically (with dry-cell batteries powering a small electric motor) or by a kerosene engine, similar to the engines used in model airplanes. They are controlled—started, stopped, and steered—by separate handheld units that beam radio signals to a receiver aboard the model. The operator can stand in one spot and run the ship or boat for quite some distance, depending upon the strength of the sending signal in the radio-control unit, as well as upon several other factors.

RC ships and boats are exciting to sail for many reasons. Their success or failure often depends on the skill of the operator, just like life-size vessels at sea. In a race, for example, a wrong turn of the rudder or steering into another boat's wake could cost the operator a victory. On a pleasure cruise, one wrong move could capsize the model, sending it to the bottom of the lake, river, or pond.

Unlike radio-controlled cars, which are most often built in either 1:8 or 1:12 scales, RC ships and boats can be built in

RC boat and transmitter

any scale, as long as the finished model is large enough and buoyant enough to carry the extra weight of the running gear and receiver. Years ago, when batteries and motors were much heavier than they are today, it was often necessary to increase the draft of a ship (the depth of the hull from the waterline to the keel) to accommodate the power system.

Today, though, the available lightweight running gear (those components within the hull that help make the model move) make it possible to motorize just about any seaworthy model. So it's common to see RC model ships and boats in scales from 1:750 up to the giant 1 inch:1 foot models, sometimes measuring 4 to 5 feet (1 to 1.5 m) in length and more than 1 foot (.3 m) at the beam (the maximum width of the vessel).

Fuel-powered RC boats feature engines that burn a type of fuel that is a cross between gasoline and kerosene. While they're the closest thing to the engines powering many of today's full-sized racing machines, their operation is anything but simple. To start one, an auxiliary motor is required. Also, filling the fuel tank can be messy and even dangerous if the operator doesn't take recommended precautions.

Far better for most modelers—and *all* beginning RC operators—are electric-powered models that feature fast-charge batteries that are ready to go in about fifteen minutes. Electric-powered ships and boats also run quieter and without annoying fumes. And it's simpler to install electric running gear than a gas system.

A third type of RC boat operates somewhat differently. Usually, it's an electric-powered model with an *impulse-type* radio rather than the digitally proportional radio common to most RC models. The impulse-type boat is capable of operating only wide open. That is, it has one speed—full forward—and can turn only fully left or fully right. It lacks the maneuverability of the digitally proportional radio boats and thus is most often considered a toy, rather than a quality RC model.

All RC ships and boats are controlled by a handheld radio transmitter. Usually the transmitter will put out radio signals on two or three channels, meaning it can control two or three entirely different functions on a single model. A two-channel unit can be used to control the steering of the ship by one signal and the speed by another.

Transmitters operate much the way a home radio does. In order for an RC transmitter to send a signal that your ships can "use," it must be tuned to the same frequency as the ship's receiver. This is done with the use of crystals. Matching crystals must be used in the ship's receiver and in the operator's transmitter. These crystals are obtained from wherever the RC ship is purchased. There are nineteen different frequencies available for RC modeling. As a rule, unless you request specific frequencies, the dealer who sells you your system will select a frequency for you.

Since the normal power of an RC transmitter is less than 100 milliwatts, no special license is required for its operation. If a stronger radio sending unit were used, however, the FCC (Federal Communications Commission) would require that the operator apply for a special license. (It's a good idea to check your local town or city ordinances, though, because in some areas there are certain times of the day during which RC boaters are restricted from operating their craft in order to prevent excessive radio wave interference.)

After you've built your first RC model ship or boat, you may well want to show it off and possibly enter it into competition with other RC models from around your area. Part of the fun of RC modeling is pitting your own vessel against other vessels featuring different hull designs and running gear, and then finding out which one comes in first.

There are many RC enthusiasts' groups all around the country, and many of these groups sponsor local, regional, and even national competitions. If you're interested in learning more about some of these groups, check out the names of some of the organizations listed in the back of this book. Ask your local hobby shop dealer, as well as other RC model hobbyists, for their recommendations.

But above all, whether you build strictly for your own enjoyment or for the thrill of hull-to-hull competition, take pride in the work you do on your model ships and boats. Learn your craft well, for it could lead to a hobby you'll enjoy for the rest of your life.

APPENDIX

The following list contains books geared both to the model ship and boat builder, as well as to the general ship enthusiast.

Benson, Brian. *Ships.* New York: Grosset & Dunlap, 1973. A general history of ships and sailing from earliest craft through modern hovercraft.

Zadig, Ernest A. *The Complete Book of Boating.* Englewood Cliffs, NJ: Prentice-Hall, 1972. Probably the best book on sailing ever written, it includes invaluable information for the model builder on ship design, running gear, galley equipment, topside and interior arrangements, and sailing techniques.

For plans of American-built ships, contact The Smithsonian Institution in Washington, D.C. They have a vast collection of plans of ships from the Revolutionary period down to the present. Write to Curator, Division of Transportation, Smithsonian Institution, Washington, D.C. 20560.

Some other maritime museums from which plans and other useful information may be had:

Chesapeake Bay Maritime Museum
PO Box 636
St. Michaels, MD 21663

Franklin D. Roosevelt Library and Museum
Albany Post Rd.
Hyde Park, NY 12538

Museum of Science and Industry
57th St. and Lake Shore Drive
Chicago, IL 60637

Nantucket Whaling Museum
c/o Nantucket Historical Association
PO Box 1016
Nantucket Island, MA 02554

Queen Mary Museum
PO Box 8
Long Beach, CA 90801

San Francisco Maritime Museum
Foot of Polk St.
San Francisco, CA 94109

American Merchant Marine Museum
c/o U.S. Merchant Marine Academy
Kings Point, NY 11024

U.S. Naval Academy Museum
Annapolis, MD 21402

U.S. Naval Museum, Building 76
Navy Yard Annex, U.S. Naval Station
Washington, D.C. 20390

One bimonthly magazine is designed exclusively for the scale-model ship builder. A typical issue may have information on RC contests, shipbuilding competitions, finishing boats and ships for authenticity, new kits on the market, building techniques, and actual plans for building various ships from scratch.

Scale Ship Modeler, Challenge Publications, Inc., 7950 Deering Ave., Canoga Park, CA 91304 ($2.95 per issue). Available from newsstands, hobby shops, and by subscription, which costs $13.50 per year in the United States and possessions and $17.50 per year elsewhere.

The following is a list of other periodicals of interest to the model ship and boat builder.

Model Ship Builder, Box 441, Menomonee Falls, WI 53051. This is the largest circulation magazine in the field. It specializes in period static models, but it also runs some articles on RC and other maritime craft.

Model Shipwright, Greenwich SE10 9NF, England. This British quarterly is devoted to the highest principles of accuracy, scale, and authenticity in both static and RC models, mostly of British craft.

Nautical Research Journal, 6413 Dahlonega Rd., Bethesda, MD 20816. This is the quarterly journal of the Nautical Research Guild. It's devoted to the history and absolute precision modeling of researched and documented period sailing vessels. It features no articles on RC modeling, but it's highly regarded by museums in the United States and abroad in the field of static model building and general maritime crafts.

GLOSSARY

Abaft. Toward the stern or directly behind something.

Abeam. Directly off the port or starboard sides.

Afore. Ahead of. "Fore" is more commonly used.

Aft. Near the stern.

Aftermast. The aft-most mast.

Aloft. Overhead, as in a ship's rigging.

Amidships. The central area of a ship.

Astern. Aft of the ship.

Ballast. A heavy weight placed low in the hull in order to lower the ship's center of gravity.

Beam. The maximum width of a ship.

Boom. A horizontal spar at the bottom of a sail attached to the mast.

Broadside. The direction parallel to the side of the ship.

Bulkhead. The walls that divide the interior of the hull.

Bulwarks. The portion of the hull that extends above the deck. Also, the walls around the weather deck.

Carling. The short fore and aft supports between deck beams.

Catamaran. A boat with two hulls connected side by side.

Centerboard. A board that passes down through a slot in the hull in order to provide lateral resistance in the water.

Companionway. Steps leading to a cabin or salon below

deck; or a hood built over a hatchway on a weather deck.

Crow's Nest. An observation post high up on a mast.

Davit. A post, like a crane, used for hoisting anchors or boats.

Dinghy. A small, open boat.

Displacement. The weight of the ship and its contents.

Dory. A long, narrow, flat-bottomed open boat.

Draft. The depth of the hull from the waterline to the keel.

Drift. The velocity, in knots, of the water current.

Fathom. A nautical unit of depth which equals six feet (1.8m).

Fore. The forward part of the ship—before or ahead of.

Forecastle (fo'c'sle). The forward part of the hull below deck.

Foremast. The mast nearest the ship's bow.

Gaff. A spar, or mast, at the head of a four-sided sail.

Ground Tackle. The anchor and its chains, ropes, etc.

Guy. A wire supporting and steadying an upright object, such as a mast.

Halyard. A line for hoisting sails or flags.

Hatch. An opening in a deck giving access to below.

Hog. An arched hull bottom that is lower at each end than in the middle, as a hog's back.

Hogging. A condition in which the weight of a wooden structure causes its less supported ends to sag.

Inboard. A boat with engines inside the hull (as opposed to outboard). Also, anything within the vessel's hull or bulwarks.

Jacob's Ladder. A rope ladder over the side of the hull.

Jib. A triangular sail set on a stay, forward of the mast.

Keel. The vertical surface at the bottom of the hull that provides lateral resistance. Also, the boat's main timber.

Ketch. A sailboat with a mainmast and a smaller mizzenmast forward of the rudder post.

Lanyard. A short piece of rope used as a handle or to secure an object.

Lazarette. The enclosed storage space at the stern of the hull below deck.

Mainsail. The principal and largest sail on a vessel.

Mainsheet. The line that controls the mainsail.

Mizzen. The shorter aftermast of a ketch, yawl, schooner, etc.

Pontoon. A float.

Port. The left side of the ship as you face forward.

Pram. A small boat with a square bow.

Rudder. A moving flat vertical surface at the stern of the boat, used to steer the boat.

Running Rigging. The lines that control the sails and yards, booms, and gaffs.

Spar. The all-inclusive name for a mast, boom, yard, etc.

Spinnaker. A large, balloon-shaped sail used at the bow of modern sailboats.

Stanchion. The post supporting a rail or a deck beam.

Strake. A length of hull planking.

Superstructure. The part of the ship above the main deck.

Tender. A small boat used to service larger craft.

Tiller. The long-leverage arm attached to the rudder post.

Truck. The top of a mast.

Trunk. The upper part of a cabin that rises through the deck.

Turnbuckle. A device with a lefthand and a righthand screw for tightening stays.

Ward Room. On naval vessels, a room reserved for use by commissioned officers.

Wheel. The steering wheel.

Yardarm. The horizontal crosspiece near the top of a mast.

Yawl. A sailing ship with a mizzenmast aft of the rudder post, in addition to a mainmast.

INDEX

Admiral Scheer, 22
Agamemnon, HMS, 5
Aircraft carriers, 11
Alecto, HMS, 6
Alfred the Great, 4
American Merchant Marine Museum, 56
Arizona, USS, 12

Ballast, 36
Benson, Brian, 55
Bismarck, 43
Blue Devil, USS, 17
Books, 55
Bounty, HMS, 16
British. *See* England
Brushes, paint, 26–28, 44, 45–47

Canoes, dugout, 2
Cement, plastic, 29–31. *See also* Glue
Charlotte Dundas, 6
Chesapeake Bay Marine Museum, 56
Chromed parts, 42–44
Clermont, The, 6

Complete Book of Boating, The (Zadig), 55
Coracles, 2
Cutty Sark, 7

Decals, 47–48
Depth charges, 9
Dragon Ships, 4
Dugout canoes, 2
Duke of York, HMS, 22

Egyptians, ancient, 2, 3
Electric power, 52–53
Elmer's® glue, 37
Emery boards, 25
Engines, 52
England (British), 4–6, 9
Escort carriers, 11

Files, 25
Flying Cloud Clipper, 16
Forecastle, 4
Forrestal, USS, 12
France, 5–6, 9
Fuel-powered models, 52
Fulton, Robert, 6

Germany, 9–11
Glue for wooden model, 37. *See also* Cement.

Hobby knives, 25, 28, 32
Hood, HMS, 43
Hornet, USS, 12

Iberia, 9
Impulse-type radios, 52–53

Japanese, 11

King George V, HMS, 30
Knives, 25, 28, 32

Lacquer, 44
Lettering, 47–48
Lexington, USS, 30
Liners, 9
Log boats, 1–2
Logos, 48
Lusitania, 21

Magazines and periodicals, 56–57
Magic Masker, 44
Masking, before painting, 44
Masking tape, 26, 44
Metalflake® paint, 44
"Miss Budweiser," 17
Missouri, USS, 30
Model cement, 29–31
Modeling putty, 26, 32
Model Ship Builder magazine, 57
Model Shipwright quarterly, 57
Motorized models, 15, 18, 34. *See also* RC models
Musashi, 22
Museum of Science and Industry, 56
Museums, maritime, 55–56

Nantucket Whaling Museum, 56
Napoleon, 5
Napoleonic Wars, 5
Nautical Research Journal, 57
Needle-nosed pliers, 26
Nelson, Horatio, 5–6
Normandie, 9

Paddles, 3
Paddle wheels, 6
Painting and finishing, 26–28, 38–48
Papyrus rafts, 2
Pearl Harbor, 11
Pennsylvania, USS, 22
Pinstriping, 47
Plans, ship, 55–56
Plastic models, 15, 24–32. *See also* Painting and finishing
Pliers, needle-nosed, 26
Pole power, 3
Polly-S, 45
Portugal, 4, 5
Prefab models, 34
Propellers, 6
PT-109, 17
Putty, 26, 32

Quarterdeck, 4
Queen Mary Museum, 56

Radio controls. *See* RC models
Rafts, papyrus, 2
Rattler, HMS, 6
Razor knives. *See* Hobby knives
RC models, 18–19, 34, 49–53
and scale, 20
Robert E. Lee, 8
Roosevelt, Franklin D., Library and Museum, 56
Rubber bands, 26

Rudder, 18–19

Sails, 3, 9
    models with, 15
Sandpaper, 25, 31
San Francisco Maritime Museum, 56
Santa Maria, 16
Scale, 20–23, 52
Scale Ship Modeler magazine, 57
Scandinavian ships, 3–4
Scharnhorst, 30
Scissors, 26
Scotland, 6
Ship-of-the-line, 5
Ships (Benson), 55
Smithsonian Institution, 55
Sobo® glue, 37
Spackling compound, 26
Spain, 4, 5
Spray boxes, 39–41
Spray guns, 41—42
Spray painting, 39–44
Static models, 15, 18, 34
    for RC models, 19
Steam power, 6–9
Submarines, 9, 11
Superstructure, 36

Tape, masking, 26, 44

Tapestripe®, 47
Tirpitz, 43
Titanic, 10
Titebond® glue, 37
Toothpicks, 26
Trafalgar, battle of, 6
Tramps, 9
Tweezers, 26

U-boats, 9
U.S. Naval Academy Museum, 56
U.S. Naval Museum, 56

Victory, HMS, 16
Viking ships, 6

White glue, 37
Wooden boats and ships, 6–8
Wooden models, 14–15, 33–37.
    See also Painting and finishing
Wood glue, 37
World War I, 9
World War II, 9–11

X-Acto knives, 25

Yankee *Sea Witch*, 27
Yorktown, USS, 46

Zadig, Ernest A., 55

ABOUT THE AUTHOR

D. J. Herda, who lives in
Blue Mounds, Wisconsin,
is a full-time writer.

His other books published
by Franklin Watts include
Model Railroads,
Model Cars and Trucks,
and *Roller Skating.*